I0802752

The Classic Edition

A Child's Garden of Bible Stories

Old Testament Workbook

Primary Level

CONCORDIA PUBLISHING HOUSE • SAINT LOUIS

Editor: Carolyn S. Bergt

This publication may be available in braille, in large print, or on cassette tape for the visually impaired. Please allow 8 to 12 weeks for delivery. Write to the Library for the Blind, 1333 S. Kirkwood Road, St. Louis, MO 63122-7295; call 1-800-433-3954, ext. 1322; or e-mail to blind.library@lcms.org.

Adapted from the Concordia Primary Religion Series, copyright ©1950 CPH
3558 S. Jefferson Avenue, St. Louis, MO 63118-3968
Manufactured in the United States of America

1 2 3 4 5 6 7 8 9 10 12 11 10 09 08 07 06 05 04 03

Contents

To Parents and Teachers

This is a workbook of activities to accompany the book *A Child's Garden of Bible Stories.* Suggestions for use and ideas for expanding concepts are given at the bottom of each page. A Web site on the Internet or the printed answer key will provide the answers if you want to reconfirm them.

Please adapt these materials to the needs and abilities of your children. For some children, you will want to read the text to them and let them dictate answers for you to write, but be sure to involve them in coloring pictures or circling choices. If some children need less assistance, make this a joint project. You may also find that some children will be able to work independently. The significant factor is that together you discuss the new life and salvation we have through Jesus Christ.

If you would like an appropriate program for memorizing Scripture and parts of the catechism, you may want to order the memory books that accompany the Voyages curriculum. These individual books for children are available inexpensively from Concordia Publishing House for kindergarten and grades 1 through 8.

As together you share the Gospel good news, rejoice in the saving grace of God's love through Christ Jesus as seen throughout all of Scripture and in our lives today!

God Makes the World

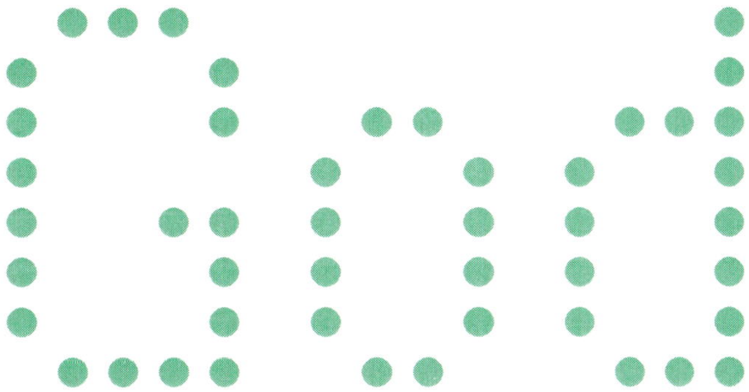

Directions

(*A Child's Garden* Bible storybook, pp. 11–13.) Ask children to say their names, and, if they are able, to write them. Ask for the name of the One who made all things. Have them trace over the word *God* with a finger and then with a crayon. Circle pictures of things God made in the six days of creation. Point out that though the other things are "man-made," the materials come from God's creation (like the wood for the chair). Draw a big circle around the entire set of pictures, remembering that all good things we have are blessings from God.

God Makes the World

Lord

heavens	heaven	earth

"In the beginning God created the

____

and the ________________."

"I believe in God, the Father Almighty, Maker of

____

and

________________________."

Directions

(*A Child's Garden* Bible storybook, pp. 11–13.) God has several names just like we do. Trace over the name *Lord* with a finger and then a crayon. Ask what other names of God the children know. Next, write the words from the answer box in the blanks to complete the sentences from Genesis 1:1 and from the First Article of the Apostles' Creed. As a reminder of the best blessing God has given us, draw a cross in the circle. Point out that God is good and perfect, but we aren't good or perfect because of sin. So God gave us Jesus, His own Son, to take away our sins.

God Makes the World

God made the world in

- six days.
- four days.
- two weeks.

First God made

- animals.
- light.
- birds.

Last of all God made

- animals.
- light.
- people.

On the seventh day God

- rested.
- started over.
- went away.

Everything God made was

- bad.
- pretty good.
- very good.

God gives us many things because

- we are good.
- He loves us.
- we are bad.

We show our thanks to God by

- praising God and obeying Him.
- taking good care of His good gifts.
- sharing what we have with others.

Directions

(*A Child's Garden* Bible storybook, pp. 11–13.) Discuss the picture by asking these questions: What did God make? For whom did He make it? Why did He make it? How could He make it? Read the statements below the picture and circle the correct ending to each sentence. Point out that in the last sentence all three answers are ways we can show our thanks to God. But we have trouble doing each of those things. We know, however, that Jesus forgives us and the Holy Spirit guides us to grow in faith, living more each day as children of God.

The First Home

Eve **A**dam **G**arden

The first man was ◯.

The first woman was ◯.

God made ◯ from the dust of the ground.

God made ◯ from a bone from ◯.

The home of ◯ and ◯ was a ◯.

When God made ◯ and ◯, they were holy.

◯ and ◯ were happy in the ◯ called Eden.

God visited with ◯ and ◯ in the ◯.

Directions

(*A Child's Garden* Bible storybook, pp. 14–15.) Study the key words below the picture. Complete the sentences by writing the beginning letter of the answer in each circle. Explain that Adam and Eve's first home was a garden prepared by God. They didn't need a house of wood or bricks to protect them from bad weather, harm, or danger because everything God had made was good and perfect. Sin changed that for everyone. But because Jesus died on the cross to take away our sin, someday all believers in Him will live in heaven, where once again everything will be good and perfect as God intended.

The First Home

When I Go to Sleep

When I Hear God's Word

When I Am Afraid

When It Is Mealtime

When I'm Sorry

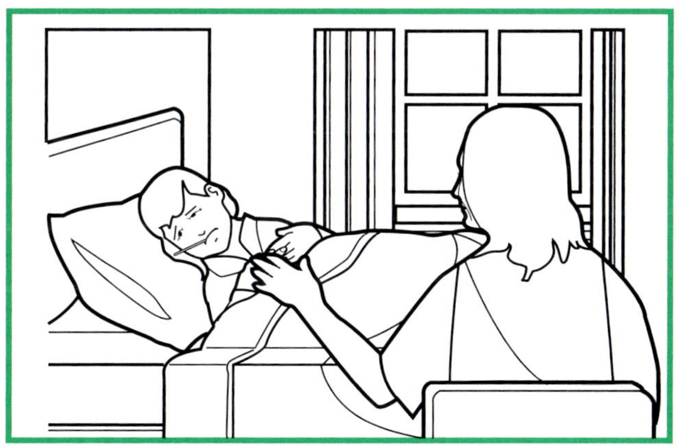

When I Feel Sick

Directions

(*A Child's Garden* Bible storybook, pp. 14–15.) Emphasize that God was with Adam and Eve in the Garden of Eden. We can be sure He is also with us in our homes today. Adam and Eve could talk with God. We can talk to God, too, in prayer. Discuss each of the pictured situations. What could you say to God in prayer at these times? Make a list of things to talk about in prayer right now. Include these thoughts as you pray together.

The First Home

____________ Love one another.

____________ Push each other.

____________ Pray to God.

____________ Help Mother.

____________ Hear God's Word.

____________ Cry and pout.

____________ Pretend you don't hear when Mom calls you.

____________ Take toys away from others.

____________ Be kind to each other.

____________ Let others play with your games.

____________ Do what Dad tells you to do.

Directions

(*A Child's Garden* Bible storybook, pp. 14–15.) Adam and Eve were happy in the home God gave to them. God blesses our homes too. They can be happy places to live when we live as children of God. This happens as Jesus justifies us, calling us to repentance and the forgiveness He offers us. This happens as the Holy Spirit sanctifies us, strengthening our faith and faith life through God's Word and Sacraments. Draw a little house on the lines beside those statements that tell about God's will for our lives as His justified and sanctified children.

The First Sin

One Tree Is Forbidden by God

Eve Listens to the Serpent

Adam Takes Fruit from Eve

SIN

Did **Wrong**

Did Not **Obey**

Directions

(*A Child's Garden* Bible storybook, pp. 16–18.) Let the children use the pictures to retell the first part of the Bible story—the first sin. Children may then trace over the dotted lines with crayon as you talk about two kinds of sin: (1) They did wrong, a sin of *commission,* which is doing what you should not do; (2) They did not obey, a sin of *omission,* which is not doing what you should do. Give examples of things people do today that are similar types of sin (for example, commission—hurting someone; omission—not helping someone who is hurt).

The First Sin

Ashamed, They Try to Hide

They Are Sent Away from the Garden

Because of their sin they had

Pain **and** Problems.

Because of God's love, He gave

a Promise.

Directions

(*A Child's Garden* Bible storybook, pp. 16–18.) Continue reviewing the Bible story, examining the illustrations, and tracing over the dotted words. Explain that consequences are results that happen because of something we do. Discuss the pain and problems we still have today because we are sinners in a sin-filled world. Emphasize, however, that this is not the end of the story, because God's love is greater than sin, death, and the devil. God promised Adam and Eve, you and me, and all the world a Savior to rescue us!

The First Sin

We Sin against Other People

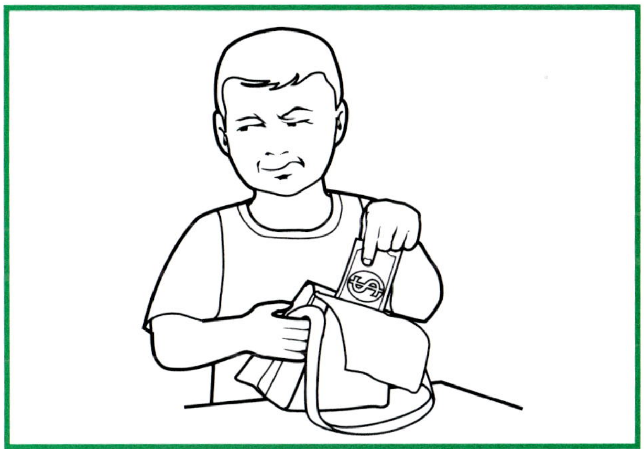

Other People Sin against Us

The Whole World Has Troubles

Directions

(*A Child's Garden* Bible storybook, pp. 16–18.) The story of Adam and Eve is also our story, because we, too, are sinners in a sin-damaged world. But in all this there is hope—the one and only hope, which we have in Jesus through His death on the cross and resurrection. Jesus calls us to faith and repentance, offering forgiveness and salvation. Have children print the word *REPENT* in the boxes going down as you spell the word. Have them print the word *HAPPY* going across, noting that true happiness is found only in the peace that comes from the loving grace of God.

The Promised Savior

_____ loved Adam and Eve.

_____ loves you and me.

_____ loves all people.

That's why ________________________ promised to send a Savior to take away our sins.

Directions

(*A Child's Garden* Bible storybook, p. 19.) Though sin had a beginning, God's love has no ending. His plan and His promise were immediate. Though Jesus would not come in the flesh till centuries later, He is central to the Old Testament. This is the purpose of Scripture—to show us our salvation in Christ Jesus. Adam and Eve's story is connected directly to Jesus, as is true in each Old Testament story and throughout history to eternity! Continue to focus on God's Gospel and grace in each lesson.

The Promised Savior

Sin makes boys and girls do things that are wrong. Sin makes grown-ups do things that are wrong. Circle the picture of the people doing wrong things.

Sin brings troubles and makes us unhappy. The love of Jesus brings hope and makes us happy. Circle the people who are happy.

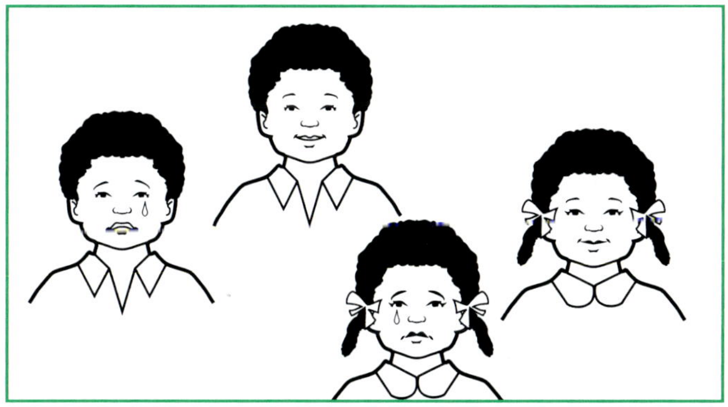

God sent Jesus to take away our sin. He died and arose for us. Circle the picture where Jesus is taking our punishment in our place.

We love Jesus because He took away our sin. We want to hear His Word. Circle the place where we go to worship Him.

Directions

(*A Child's Garden* Bible storybook, p. 19.) Adapt your procedures to the needs and abilities of the children. If they can read well and can proceed on their own, that is fine, but be ready to assist them and always follow up with group discussion. However, if the text is difficult for some children, by all means read it aloud for them. These activities should not be a test of reading skills. Reading progress should not become an obstacle to learning about Jesus. Focus on a joy-filled application of God's Word to the life of each child.

The Promised Savior

Son of God	Jesus	is the
Jesus died	of the world	for the sins
Jesus	because of my sins	suffered on the cross
to forgive	our sins	We ask Jesus
love Jesus	thank and praise Him	Children who
God wants	to be saved	all people
Those who	go to heaven	believe in Jesus will

Directions

(*A Child's Garden* Bible storybook, p. 19.) Each line above contains the words needed for a sentence. But there is one group of words that is out of order in each line. Read the phrases aloud (hearing them will help comprehension). Then have children identify the phrase that is out of order, circle it, and draw an arrow to where it belongs. Reread the sentence correctly. The first one is done for you.

The Children of Adam and Eve

What Gift Does God Want?

Cain

Abel

What Can You Give to God?

(*A Child's Garden* Bible storybook, pp. 20–21.) Ask, Does God like offerings of sheep better than grain? No, what made the difference was the heart of the giver. Abel gave the first and best of what he had out of love and respect for God. Cain, putting himself first, gave what he didn't want or need. What gift does God want from us? He wants our hearts filled with faith, love, and gratitude. Draw a heart above the altar. Read about God's gifts to us in Romans 8:32. Discuss and draw gifts we can give (such as a coin, musical notes, or hands serving others—see Matthew 25:40).

Directions

The Children of Adam and Eve

Anger Can Lead To

God's Word says: "Turn away anger" (Proverbs 29:8) and "Turn to God" (Acts 3:19).

love **hate**

Jesus tells us to ______________ one another. Jesus does not want us to ____________ anyone.

love **hate**

We ___________ Jesus because He took our sins away. Because we love Him, we will __________ sin.

hurt **help**

It is a sin to ____________ people. Jesus wants us to ____________ others.

pray **prayer**

Jesus wants us to ___________. He will hear our _____________ and forgive our sins.

Directions

(*A Child's Garden* Bible storybook, pp. 20–21.) God gave Cain opportunities to confess and repent of his sins. Instead, he turned to anger. Discuss how anger, unchecked, grows into other sins such as hurtful words and actions. The Bible verses tell God's will for our lives. We are led to follow God's will as Jesus forgives our sins and the Holy Spirit works faith in us and strengthens us through God's Word. Have the children fill in the blanks with the correct words and learn more about God's will for our lives.

The Children of Adam and Eve

God's Word Calls Us to Repent

Confess

your sins.

Believe

that Jesus forgives.

Repent, then, and turn to God, so that your sins may be wiped out. Acts 3:19

What Happens Next? What Does This Mean?

LIVE 4 ✝

Directions

(*A Child's Garden* Bible storybook, pp. 20–21.) *Note: Cain did not repent. He did not confess his sins, and instead of trusting God for forgiveness, he was only concerned about the punishment.* Discuss God's will for our lives. As the children trace over the dotted lines, explain that *repent* means to *confess* (admit what we did wrong) and *believe* (trust that Jesus died on the cross to take away our sins). The result of repentance (what happens next) is that, by the power of God working in us through His Word and Sacraments, we *Live for Jesus.* Give examples of this.

The Flood

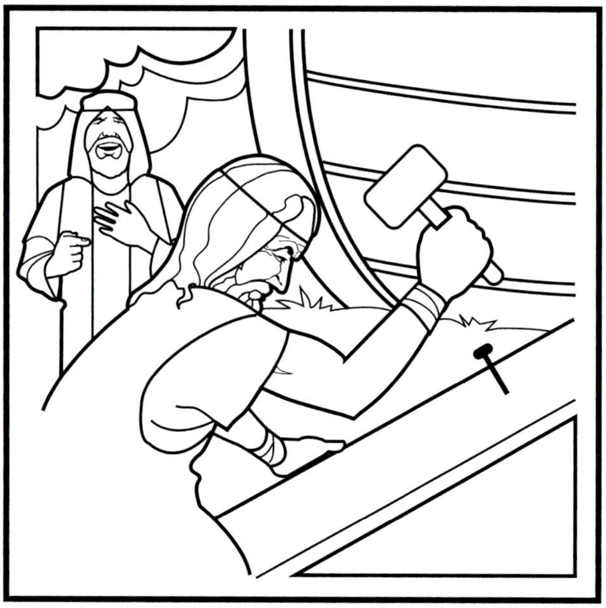

Trust God's Good Plans

Trust God Will Protect

Trust God Will Bless

Trust God Is Near

Directions

(*A Child's Garden* Bible storybook, pp. 22–23.) Have children circle the word *trust* each time they see it on the page. Even though others may have thought building a boat on dry land was silly, Noah trusted God's wisdom. Even though it stormed for more than a month, Noah trusted God would keep them safe. Even though the world was greatly changed by the flood, Noah trusted God would bless them. Draw a picture of some troubles you might have. Remember that God will do what is best for you. Pray together that God will help you faithfully trust Him.

The Flood

We know God hates sin because He sent the

Flood.

We know God loves us even though we are sinners because He sent the

Savior.

(*A Child's Garden* Bible storybook, pp. 22–23.) God is just and fair. People are sinners. Sin must be punished. If God didn't punish sin, it would suggest that He accepts it. But a just God cannot accept sin. The punishment for sin is death, eternally. (Read Romans 6:23.) But God loves us, and His love does not change. So Jesus took our sin, and Jesus took our punishment. Jesus switched places with us when He went to the cross. He took our sins and gave us His righteousness and His victory. (Read 2 Corinthians 5:21 and 1 Corinthians 15:57.) Praise God!

The Flood

GOD IS GOOD

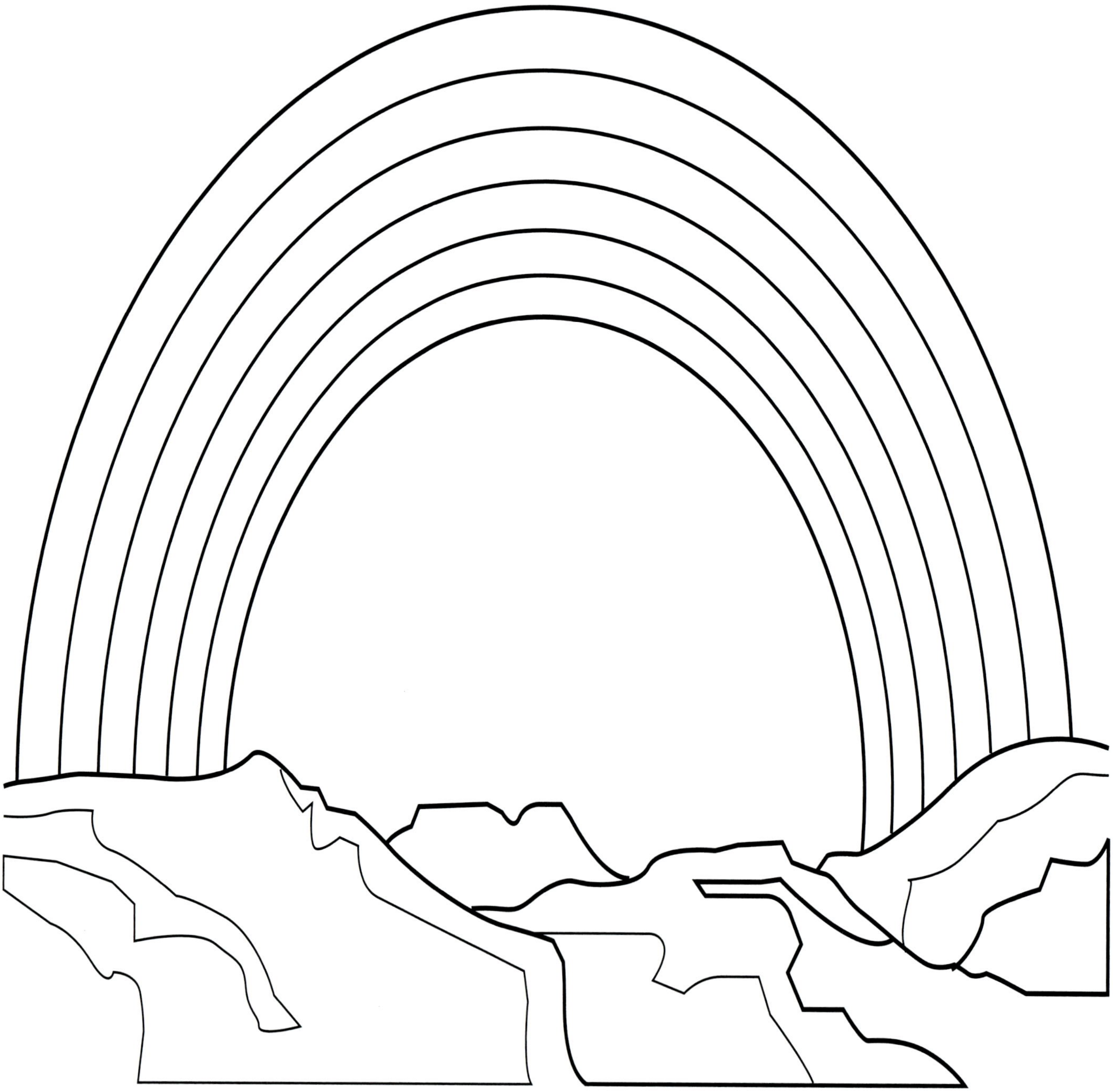

Directions

(*A Child's Garden* Bible storybook, pp. 22–23.) Have the children color the stripes of the rainbow in this order, starting at the top: red, orange, yellow, green, blue, purple. (Point out that these colors, alternating, are the primary and the secondary colors on a color wheel.) The rainbow, created by God, is a sign that reminds us that God keeps His promises—all of them. In the space below the rainbow draw a cross to remember the greatest promise God made. God kept this promise through Christ Jesus, bringing us forgiveness and eternal life.

Abraham's Faith in God

After the time of Noah, many people again forgot about the one ______ ______ ______ ______ God.

Many of them prayed to ______ ______ ______ ______ ______.

There was a man who loved God.

His name was ______ ______ ______ ______ ______ ______ ______.

God wanted him to have a new start in a new ______ ______ ______ ______.

When God told him to GO,

he ______ ______ ______ ______ ______ ______ ______ God.

God ______ ______ ______ ______ ______ ______ ______ ______

him a new home in the land of Canaan.

Abraham knew there is only ______ ______ ______ true God.

Use the words in the answer box to fill in the blanks.

idols promised one true land Abraham trusted

Directions

(*A Child's Garden* Bible storybook, pp. 24–25.) The Bible tells us that God often talked with Abraham. God called Abraham His friend. We also know that Abraham was a sinner; the Bible tells of some of his serious sins. But Abraham was blessed by God with a strong faith. Pray together for that same blessing of faith. Many times in our lives things will occur where we don't understand what is happening or why. Pray that God will help you to put the situation in His hands, trusting as Abraham did that God knows the "what" and the "why," and He will do what is best.

Abraham's Faith in God

God's List of Promises to Abraham

- ☐ A new land
- ☐ A large family
- ☐ A Savior for the world

Draw a check mark in the box before each promise that God kept.

Directions

(*A Child's Garden* Bible storybook, pp. 24–25.) God kept all of these promises. (1) He led Abraham to the new homeland of Canaan. And centuries later, after the people had moved to Egypt, God led them back to the promised land. (2) Even though Abraham and Sarah were elderly and had no children, nothing is impossible for God. Like the stars, the size of Abraham's family would become too large to count. (3) The promise of the Savior to Abraham is also a promise for all people. Read about God's faithfulness to us in Christ Jesus in 2 Corinthians 1:20.

Abraham's Faith in God

Directions

(*A Child's Garden* Bible storybook, pp. 24–25.) Have the children trace over the dotted lines with a yellow crayon to brighten the stars in the night sky. Point to the one that is different than the rest. Explain that this is actually two letters of the Greek alphabet. This is a symbol (a picture or design) that reminds us of Jesus because this is the beginning of the word *Christ* (another name for Jesus) in Greek (the language the New Testament was first written in). Look for this symbol in church, and let it remind you of the promised Savior, Jesus Christ.

Abraham and the Angels

Sarah laughed.

You are welcome here.

Visitors are coming.

God kept His promise.

Directions

(*A Child's Garden* Bible storybook, pp. 26–27.) Place the pictures in the right order by numbering them from 1 to 4. Write the numbers in the small boxes. Have the children retell the story of one of God's many promises. Point out that this baby (Isaac) would grow up to have two sons. One of them would have 12 sons, and the family would grow and grow until it was too big to count (just as God had said). And from this family, many years later, the Savior, Jesus, was born. See a list of part of this family in Matthew 1, especially verses 2 and 16.

Abraham and the Angels

One day the Lord and two angels came to visit Abraham.	Yes	No
Abraham gave shoes to the Lord and the angels.	Yes	No
The Lord said, "Sarah will have a son."	Yes	No
Sarah believed the words of God.	Yes	No
God kept His promise. The next year they had a baby boy.	Yes	No
Some things are too hard for God to do.	Yes	No
God promises that all who believe in Jesus as Savior will go to heaven.	Yes	No
God keeps just a few of His promises.	Yes	No

Directions

(*A Child's Garden* Bible storybook, pp. 26–27.) Have children circle *yes* or *no* to indicate if the statement is right or wrong. After completing the answers, discuss the incorrect ones (every other one) and change them to correct statements. (You will change *shoes* to *food; believed* to *did not believe; some things are* to *nothing is; just a few* to *all.*)

The Offering of Isaac

One day God told Abraham to

______ sacrifice a lamb.

______ sacrifice his son.

______ sacrifice a deer.

Abraham loved his son very much, but he also wanted to

______ obey God.

______ do nothing.

______ run away.

At the top of a hill Abraham

______ built a house.

______ built an altar.

______ built a boat.

Abraham said to Isaac:

______ "Are you ready?"

______ "Did you forget to bring the wood?"

______ "God will provide a lamb."

When Abraham was ready to kill his son,

______ Sarah stopped him.

______ God stopped him.

______ Isaac ran away.

God promised to bless Abraham because he had

______ been ready to give up his son.

______ not told Isaac what would happen

______ loved Isaac more than himself

Directions

(*A Child's Garden* Bible storybook, pp. 28–30.) Place a check mark before the right ending for each sentence. Explain that an offering is a good gift you give to God. A sacrifice is an offering of something that is especially important or valuable to you. In Old Testament times, the people often gave a lamb to be sacrificed on an altar. They would give their first and best. Today most people don't have lambs, so we often give money as an offering because it is something valuable to us. We give in thankfulness to God for the salvation He gives to us.

The Offering of Isaac

Directions

(*A Child's Garden* Bible storybook, pp. 28–30.) As you review the story, recall that both Abraham and Isaac were obedient to God. Obedience can be very difficult. We often fail; that is called sin. Pray together, thanking God for His forgiveness through Jesus and asking Him to help you grow in obedience to His will and ways. Note that each picture above shows obedience and disobedience. Have the children draw a line from the child at the top of each section to the picture showing the child obediently following God's ways.

The Offering of Isaac

God so loved the world that He gave His ______________________________, that whoever believes in Him shall not perish but have eternal life. John 3:16

Behold! The ______________ of God who takes away the sin of the world! John 1:29 NKJV

Directions

(*A Child's Garden* Bible storybook, pp. 28–30.) Explain that when God saw Abraham's faithfulness, He did not make Abraham sacrifice his son. But God's own love for us was so great that He willingly sacrificed His one and only Son—Jesus—to save us from our sin. Complete the second picture, drawing a cross to show where Jesus was sacrificed, giving up His life for us. That is why He is called the Lamb of God. Then look up and complete the Bible verses.

The Ladder to Heaven

(*A Child's Garden* Bible storybook, pp. 31–32.) God's blessing for Jacob is also true for us. God says in Genesis 28:15, "I am with you and will watch over you wherever you go." God also sends His holy angels to watch over us. Psalm 91:11–12 says, "He will command His angels concerning you to guard you in all your ways; they will lift you up in their hands, so that you will not strike your foot against a stone." Discuss times when, like Jacob, you may feel afraid or lonely, and emphasize God's constant care in these situations.

The Ladder to Heaven

1

2

- [ ] When Isaac was very old, he blessed his sons.
- [ ] Jacob was traveling to his uncle's house for safety.
- [ ] Esau became very angry because Jacob got the best blessing.
- [ ] Jacob became tired. He fell asleep on the ground.
- [ ] Jacob had a beautiful dream.
- [ ] One end of the ladder was on the ground and the other end in heaven.
- [ ] Esau wanted to harm Jacob.
- [ ] Isaac, Jacob, and Esau were all sinners.
- [ ] Jacob saw angels walking up and down the ladder.
- [ ] God said, "Some day the Savior will be born from your family."

Directions

(*A Child's Garden* Bible storybook, pp. 31–32.) Review what is happening in the pictures. (If you want to give extra details about the first picture, see Genesis 27.) Read each sentence and have the children write in the box if it belongs with picture 1 or 2. Point out that all three men in this Bible story were sinners; they acted according to their own will rather than God's. Though Jacob was a sinner, he realized that God had not abandoned him. When he awoke from the dream, he worshiped God for His forgiveness, care, and blessings.

The Ladder to Heaven

God was with Jacob while he was sleeping.
We need not be afraid at night—

because God is always near.

because we are strong.

Before we go to sleep, we can pray and ask God to be with us—

because we have more time at night.

because God can help us.

God will be with us—

because we are good.

because He loves and forgives us

When we wake up in the morning, we—

thank God for taking care of us.

begin to play and forget about God.

(*A Child's Garden* Bible storybook, pp. 31–32.) Read the beginning of each sentence and circle the correct ending. Discuss various aspects of prayer. It is our way to talk to God. He hears what we say and what we think (silent prayers). Some prayers are long, some are very short. God hears and answers them all. In prayer we can praise and thank God, we can confess our sins and ask for forgiveness, and we can ask God to help us and others. Whatever God's answer to prayer is (yes, wait, or "I have a better idea"), we can trust that He knows and does what is best.

Joseph and His Dreams

Do **Don't**

________ say something if it will upset others.

________ be happy when good things happen to someone else.

________ be unkind to others.

________ act as if you are better than someone else.

________ try to be a peacemaker.

________ ask God to forgive when you do wrong.

________ ask God to guide you to live as His people.

Directions

(*A Child's Garden* Bible storybook, pp. 33–34.) Ask children to draw an *X* on the two things in the picture that Joseph's brothers did not like. Discuss why they were jealous of his coat and his dreams. Print either *Do* or *Don't* on the blanks to complete the sentences correctly. Talk about Jesus' forgiveness for all sins, and pray for the Holy Spirit's power to lead us to obedience. Note that the statements are ideas to help families get along together, but they are also true for our relationships with friends, neighbors, and classmates.

Joseph and His Dreams

Hurry, let's not let him play with us.

I'm going to tear up your ugly picture.

You are just a crybaby.

I'm going to keep this all for myself.

Directions

(*A Child's Garden* Bible storybook, pp. 33–34.) Discuss each picture. These people need God's forgiveness and a change of heart through the power of the Holy Spirit. Discuss what the situation would be like if this change takes place in these brothers and sisters. Cross off the caption and write a new response inside the speech balloon to indicate behavior that is guided by God's love. *(Possibilities: Hurry, we'll wait for you to catch up. Maybe I can repair this picture for you. Don't cry—I'll help you. Want to share this?)*

Joseph Is Sold

God had a ________________ for Joseph.

God has a ________________ for me.

God has a ________________ through Jesus

So we'll live eternally.

Directions

(*A Child's Garden* Bible storybook, pp. 35–37.) The poem tells about three of God's plans. (Print *plan* in each blank.) First, though things at this point looked bad for Joseph, God had a plan to use him to bless many people. Assure the children that God has a good plan for each of them. Even as we face problems and troubles, God can bless us. (Read together Jeremiah 29:11.) And then consider God's greatest and ultimate plan for us through Jesus' death and resurrection—rescuing us from sin, death, and Satan and giving us forgiveness, life, and salvation.

Joseph Is Sold

God Talks to Me

We know that in all things God works for the good of those who love Him. Romans 8:28

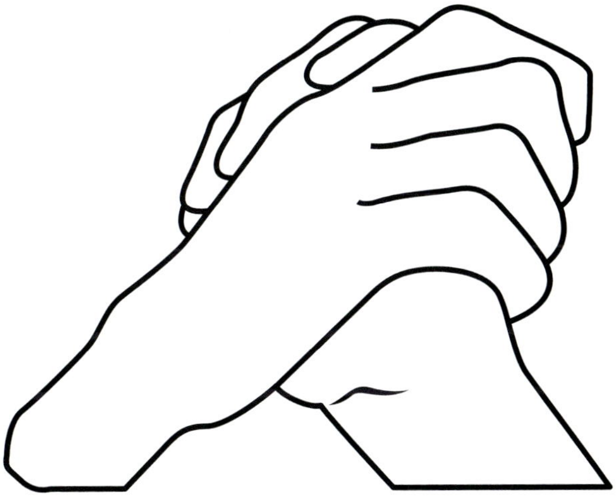

I Talk to God

Directions

(*A Child's Garden* Bible storybook, pp. 35–37.) Have each child dictate a prayer to be written here by a teacher or parent. Then pray the prayer together, knowing that God will hear and answer. God will do what is best and at the time that is best because He has all power and knows all things. Praise God!

Joseph Rules over Egypt

plan	slave	help	lies	blessed	forgot

Joseph went to Egypt because he was sold as a ___________________.

Joseph went to jail because someone told ________________ about him.

Joseph stayed in jail because someone ___________________ about him.

Joseph went to the king's palace. This was part of God's _____________.

Joseph explained the king's dreams because of God's _____________.

Joseph became a wise ruler because God ____________________ him.

Directions

(*A Child's Garden* Bible storybook, pp. 38–39.) We are sinners living in a sinful world. We will have troubles. Things happen that seem unjust and unfair. But God is always near. In the midst of tragedy, God can bring blessing. Look at the tragedy of Jesus on the cross. From that, God brought the greatest blessings—forgiveness, life, and salvation—for us. Always remember the comforting words of Isaiah 41:13, "I am the LORD, your God, who takes hold of your right hand and says to you, Do not fear; I will help you."

Joseph Rules over Egypt

KING: What does my dream mean?

JOSEPH: ______________________________

____

KING: What should we do?

JOSEPH: ______________________________

____

In what ways was **JOSEPH** now treated like a **KING**?

____

____

Directions

(*A Child's Garden* Bible storybook, pp. 38–39.) Have the children color the illustrations, contrasting between the years of plenty and the years of famine. In the first two sections give Joseph's response to the king. In the last one list ways Joseph was treated like a king. Which of these relates to Joseph's own dream? When discussing Joseph's wise plan, also discuss how we today can wisely prepare for the future (for example, don't waste, have a savings account, and above all, always pray for and rely on God's guidance and blessing).

The Brothers Go to Egypt

We have come to buy food.

I am your brother Joseph.

Have mercy on us, sir.

Jacob, my father! Welcome!

Directions

(*A Child's Garden* Bible storybook, pp. 40–42.) Have the children use the pictures to retell this part of Joseph's story. You may use this as a guide to help the children act out the Bible story. If you want to explore more of the details, read Genesis 41–45.

The Brothers Go to Egypt

I AM SORRY.

I FORGIVE YOU.

Directions

(*A Child's Garden* Bible storybook, pp. 40–42.) Children may add color or designs to the letters on this page to direct attention to them. Point out that these words are easy to spell but hard to say. Ask what makes these words so difficult. (Too often we don't want to admit we've done something wrong. And too often our first impulse is to hurt back and get even rather than forgive.) We can look at Joseph, led by his faith in God, as an example of forgiveness. But the best example is Jesus Himself on the cross. Read together Luke 23:34 and Colossians 3:13.

Moses, the Leader of God's People

God had special plans
for this baby
in a basket.
One day Moses
would lead
God's people
from Egypt to
Canaan,
the promised land.

God had special plans
for this baby
in a manger.
One day Jesus
would lead
God's people
from sin
to salvation.

Directions

(*A Child's Garden* Bible storybook, pp. 43–45.) Point out that more than a thousand years separated these two Bible stories. Discuss why the story of Jesus is so much more important.

Emphasize that Jesus is God's own Son. He gave up His life to save us. And He leads us to a greater promised land—in heaven!

Moses, the Leader of God's People

I was afraid the Children of Israel would get too powerful.

I made them work very hard as slaves.

I sent my soldiers to kill the baby boys.

Who am I?

Moses Princess King

My mother loved me very much.

She did not want the king to hurt me.

She hid me in a floating basket.

A princess found me.

Who am I?

King Miriam Moses

I loved my little boy Moses very much.

I wanted to protect him.

I hid Moses from the king's soldiers.

God's plan returned baby Moses to me.

Who am I?

Princess Moses Mother

I was covered with tar to keep water out.

I was put in the tall grass near the river.

Baby Moses slept in me.

They brought me to the princess.

Who am I?

Moses Basket Pharaoh

I hid near the river.

I watched baby Moses.

I did not want anyone to hurt him.

I brought my mother to care for the baby.

Who am I?

Brother Sister Princess

I was the king's daughter.

I came to the river.

I saw a little basket and opened it.

I loved the tiny baby.

Who am I?

Nile Princess Mother

Directions

(*A Child's Garden* Bible storybook, pp. 43–45.) Together read the riddles and circle the correct answers. Let the children make up similar Bible story riddles of their own. Look at three words on this page that were not previously discussed: explain that *Miriam* is Moses' sister; *Pharaoh* is what the kings of Egypt were called; and *Nile* is the name of the river where Moses' basket boat was placed.

Moses, the Leader of God's People

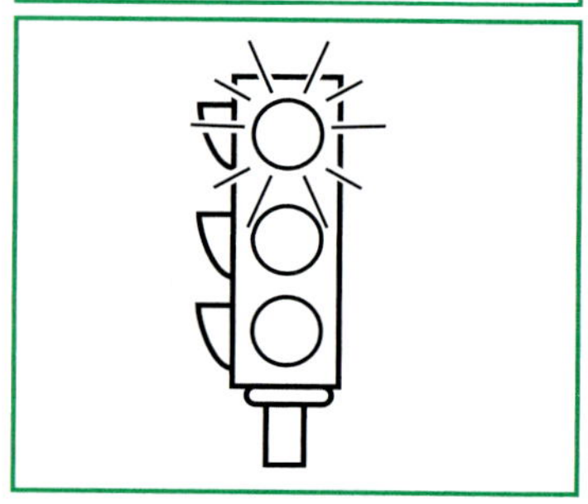

Directions

(*A Child's Garden* Bible storybook, pp. 43–45.) God protected Moses; God protects us. God blessed Moses through many helpers, such as his mother and sister. God blesses us through many helpers today. Draw a line from the pictures of places where we need help to the one who helps in that situation. In prayer, thank God for blessing us through these helpers. Thank God for the many gifts of protection He gives to us each day. And thank Him for the greatest protection we have through Jesus, who protects us from the dangers of sin, death, and Satan.

The Children of Israel Leave Egypt

Who Said:

"It is time for My people to return."

"I want you to be their leader."

"Who will do our hard work?"

"God wants you to let my people go."

"I will not obey your God."

"I will send a powerful angel."

"Go before your God kills us all."

"It is time for us to go."

"Hurry! Bring them back."

"God will help us."

"Hold your hand over the sea."

Directions

(*A Child's Garden* Bible storybook, pp. 46–47.) Read each statement and draw a circle around the picture to indicate who said it—God, Moses, or King Pharaoh. In this Bible story we see the great power of God. The king of Egypt resisted the power of God but was overwhelmed. Moses relied on the power of God and served as His prophet. It was God's power—not Moses'—that set the people free. It is only God's power through the death and resurrection of Jesus that sets us free from sin, death, and Satan.

The Children of Israel Leave Egypt

- ❑ The king (Pharaoh) would not let the Children of Israel go.
- ❑ Moses said, "God wants you to let my people stay in Egypt."
- ❑ The king said, "I will not obey your God."
- ❑ The Children of Israel put the blood of a lamb on their doors.
- ❑ The Children of Israel got ready to leave Egypt.
- ❑ The angel killed some of the Children of Israel.
- ❑ The Children of Israel obeyed God.
- ❑ The angel killed the oldest child in the Egyptian homes.
- ❑ Then the king said, "Go!"
- ❑ The Children of Israel began to march toward the Green Sea.
- ❑ The king changed his mind and wanted the people back.
- ❑ The king and his army chased after the people of Israel.
- ❑ The people of Israel were afraid.
- ❑ Moses held his hand over the water.
- ❑ God made a dry bridge over the sea.
- ❑ God was with the soldiers of the king of Egypt.
- ❑ The Children of Israel safely reached land on the other side of the sea.
- ❑ God saved His people!

Directions

(*A Child's Garden* Bible storybook, pp. 46–47.) Review these statements about God's rescue plan. Place an *X* in the box before sentences that are true. Cross off words in sentences that are wrong and talk about what they should say. (Change *stay in* to *leave; some* to *none; Green* to *Red; bridge over* to *path through; was with* to *defeated.*) You may also want to discuss the Old Testament celebration of the Passover Feast and the New Testament celebration of the Sacrament of the Lord's Supper, instituted by Christ Himself for the remission of sins.

The Children of Israel Leave Egypt

"The Lord . . . guides me in paths of righteousness" (Psalm 23:1–3)

as the Holy Spirit works through the means of grace:

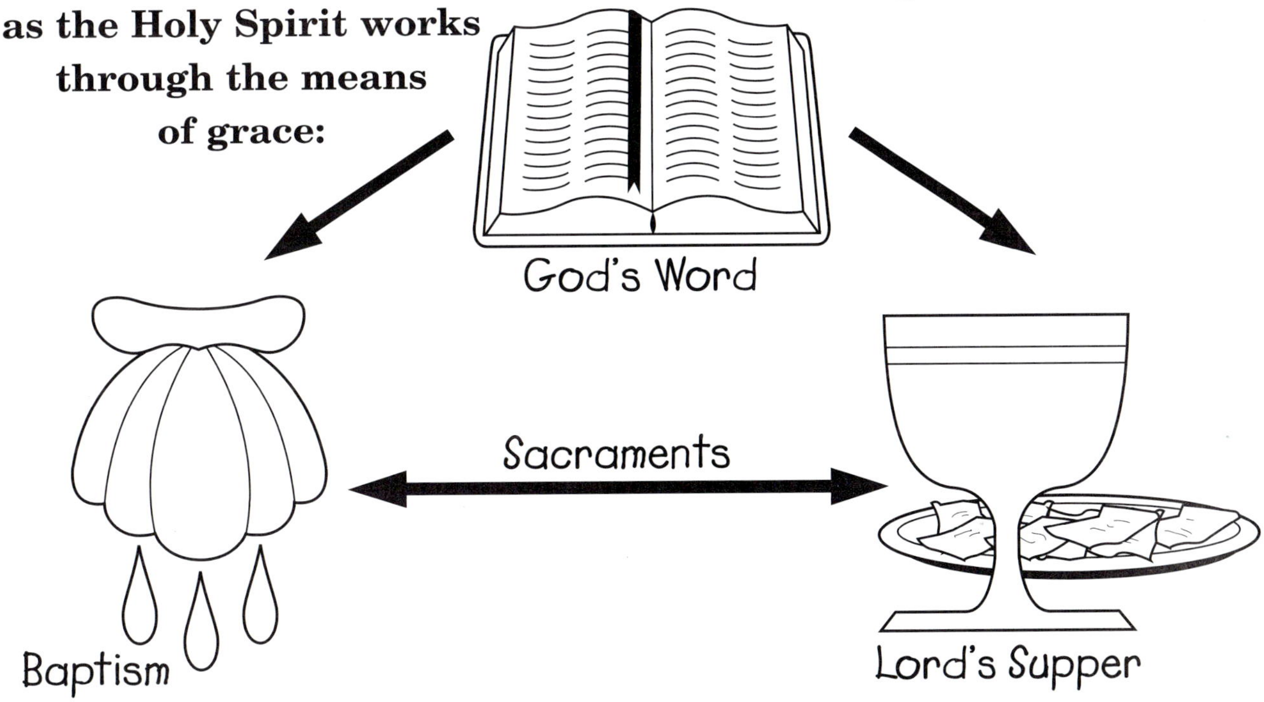

Directions

(*A Child's Garden* Bible storybook, pp. 46–47.) God chose Moses to be a leader. God blesses us today with leaders, such as Christian parents, teachers, and pastors. But the most important leader is Jesus—true God Himself—who leads us to salvation. The Holy Spirit works through the means of grace to lead us to faith and forgiveness in the name of Jesus, who died on the cross and arose at Easter for us. The means of grace—God's Word and the Sacraments (which have God's Word in them)—are God's gifts to us, offering forgiveness and eternal life in Jesus.

The Golden Calf

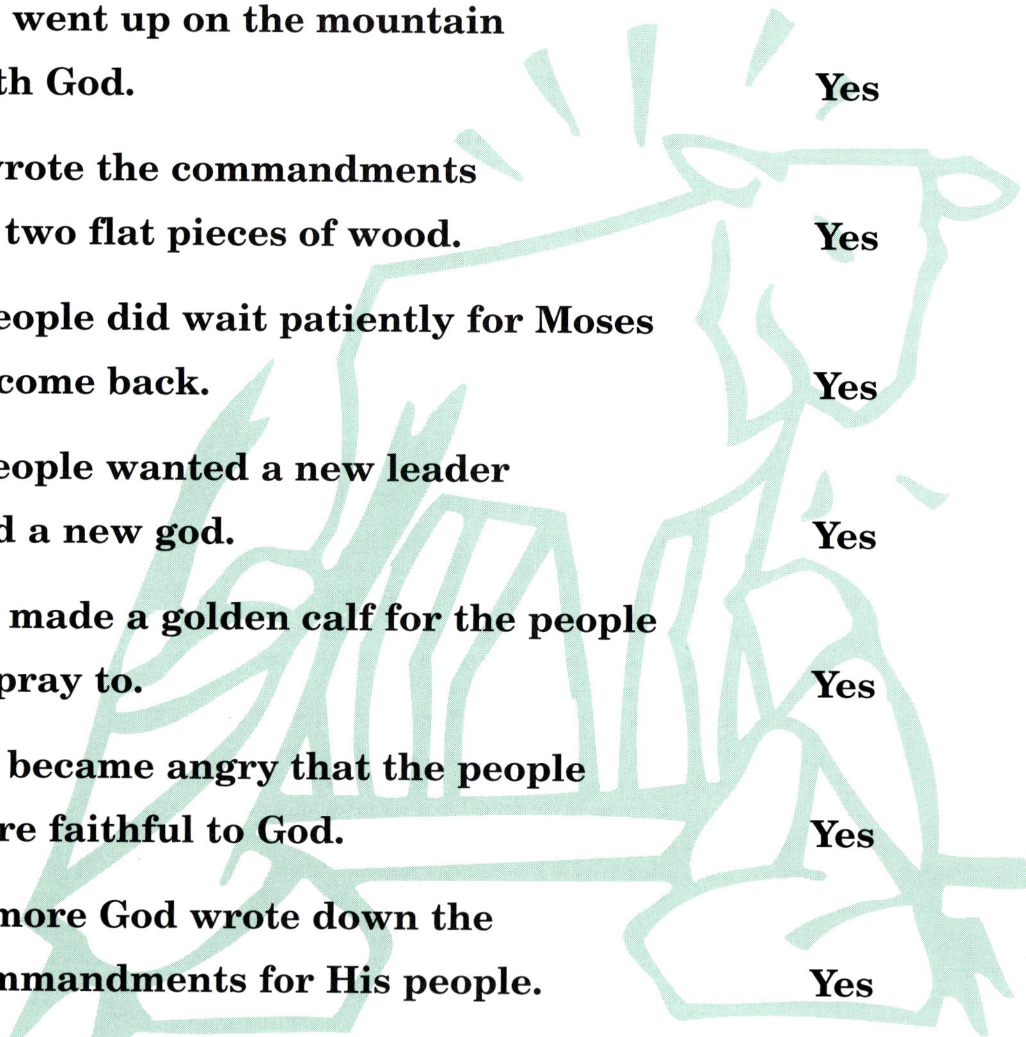

God gave the commandments on Mount Sinai.	Yes	No
Aaron went up on the mountain with God.	Yes	No
God wrote the commandments on two flat pieces of wood.	Yes	No
The people did wait patiently for Moses to come back.	Yes	No
The people wanted a new leader and a new god.	Yes	No
Aaron made a golden calf for the people to pray to.	Yes	No
Moses became angry that the people were faithful to God.	Yes	No
Once more God wrote down the commandments for His people.	Yes	No
Moses taught the Twelve Commandments to the people.	Yes	No

Directions

(*A Child's Garden* Bible storybook, pp. 48–49.) Read the sentences and then circle *yes* or *no* to indicate if a sentence is right or wrong. Discuss changes that need to be made to the wrong sentences to make them correct. Words to change are *Aaron, wood, did, faithful, Twelve.* Point out that it is God's will that we obey His commandments. But He knows that we can't because we are sinners (like the Children of Israel). So He sends Jesus to forgive our sins, and He sends the Holy Spirit to grow and strengthen our faith in Jesus and His salvation. To God be the glory!

The Golden Calf

Luke 10:27

Love the Lord your God with all your heart and with all your soul and with all your strength and with all your mind.

Love your neighbor as yourself.

1. *Don't* let anything be more important to you than God.
2. *Don't* say God's name as a curse word.
3. *Don't* play instead of hearing God's Word.
4. *Don't* disobey your mother and father.
5. *Don't* hurt other people.
6. *Don't* disrespect each other as boys or girls.
7. *Don't* take what belongs to someone else.
8. *Don't* say bad things about other people.
9. *Don't* wish you could have what belongs to someone else.
10. *Don't* plan to harm other people's friendships.

Do be content with what is yours.

Do help people keep what belongs to them.

Do be kind and helpful to others.

Do go to church to worship God.

Do love and honor God above all else.

Do thank God for blessing you with friends.

Do say kind words about other people.

Do act, think, and speak decently about others.

Do follow the instructions of your teachers.

Do use God's name to thank and praise Him.

Directions

(*A Child's Garden* Bible storybook, pp. 48–49.) God gave us the Ten Commandments for living as His people. Luke 10:27 gives us a two-part summary of those rules. The Ten Commandments give us a lot of *don'ts,* but they also suggest what we should *do.* Draw a line from the commandment summaries in the "don't list" to match them with what they imply we should do. After looking at all this, we realize we can't do any of this on our own. We live as people of God only through the forgiveness of Jesus and the power of the Holy Spirit working in us through God's Word.

Ruth

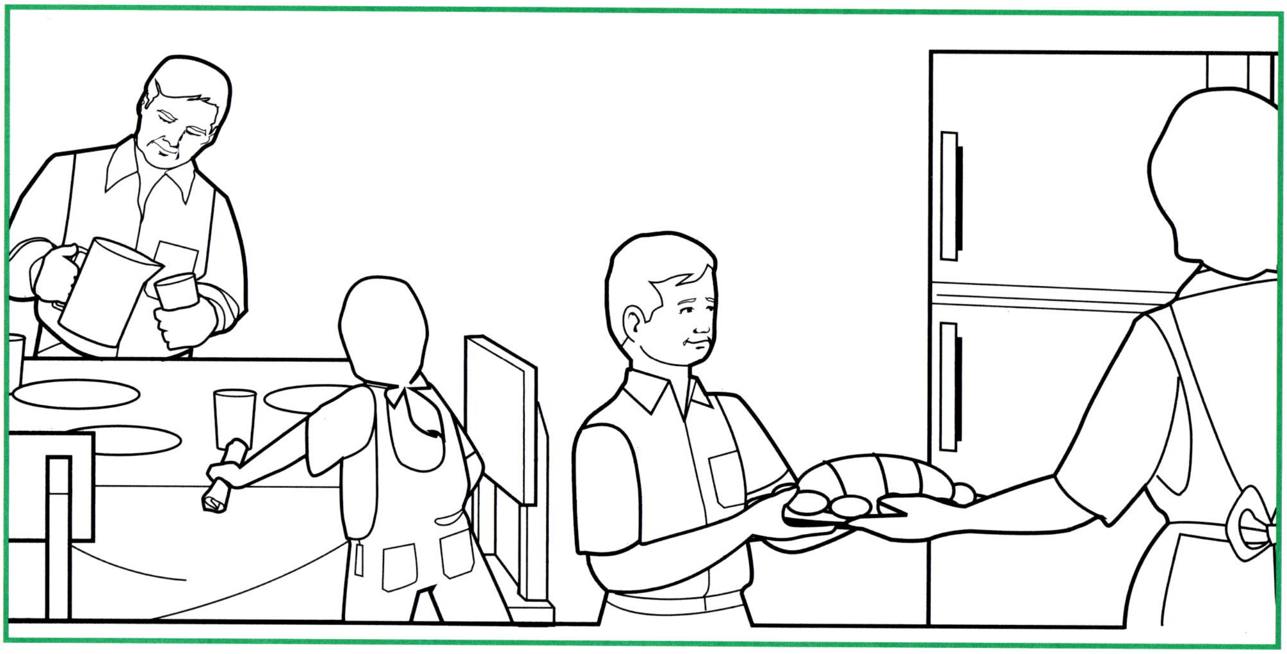

Ruth showed love to Naomi when she

went back to Bethlehem with her.

would not help Naomi.

worked in the fields for food.

I show love for my parents when

I help them with their work.

I come when they call me.

I let my toys lie all over the floor.

I show love for old people when

I give them my chair when they are standing.

I make lots of noise and run through the house.

I carry heavy boxes for them.

I show love for other boys and girls when

I want to have my way when we play.

I share my toys with them.

I am kind to them.

Directions

(*A Child's Garden* Bible storybook, pp. 52–53.) Ask the children to circle two possible answers for each sentence to indicate ways we can show love and helpfulness to others. Remind the children that we are sinners who do not always do as God wants us to. But God has the power not only to forgive our sins, but also to *transform* our lives. That means He has the power to change us so that we can grow in faith and in living as His children. As we receive the great love of Jesus, we learn to show love to others. 1 John 4:19 says, "We love because He first loved us."

The Golden Calf

Luke 10:27

Love the Lord your God with all your heart and with all your soul and with all your strength and with all your mind.

Love your neighbor as yourself.

1. *Don't* let anything be more important to you than God.
2. *Don't* say God's name as a curse word.
3. *Don't* play instead of hearing God's Word.
4. *Don't* disobey your mother and father.
5. *Don't* hurt other people.
6. *Don't* disrespect each other as boys or girls.
7. *Don't* take what belongs to someone else.
8. *Don't* say bad things about other people.
9. *Don't* wish you could have what belongs to someone else.
10. *Don't* plan to harm other people's friendships.

Do be content with what is yours.

Do help people keep what belongs to them.

Do be kind and helpful to others.

Do go to church to worship God.

Do love and honor God above all else.

Do thank God for blessing you with friends.

Do say kind words about other people.

Do act, think, and speak decently about others.

Do follow the instructions of your teachers.

Do use God's name to thank and praise Him.

Directions

(*A Child's Garden* Bible storybook, pp. 48–49.) God gave us the Ten Commandments for living as His people. Luke 10:27 gives us a two-part summary of those rules. The Ten Commandments give us a lot of *don'ts,* but they also suggest what we should *do.* Draw a line from the commandment summaries in the "don't list" to match them with what they imply we should do. After looking at all this, we realize we can't do any of this on our own. We live as people of God only through the forgiveness of Jesus and the power of the Holy Spirit working in us through God's Word.

The Golden Calf

God says

NO

to sin.

God says

YES

to all
His promises.

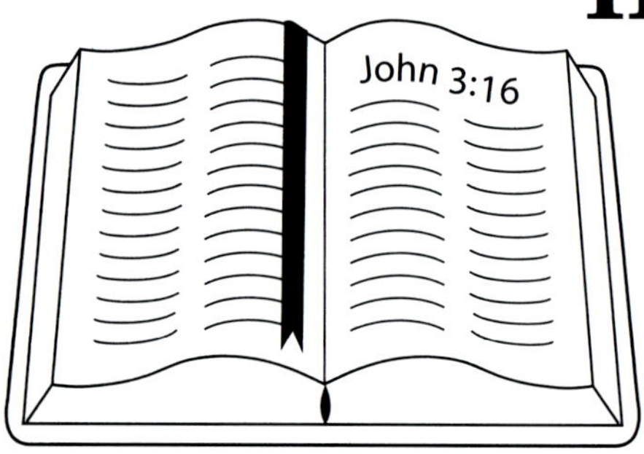

Directions

(*A Child's Garden* Bible storybook, pp. 48–49.) Draw a line from the word *NO* to the pictures showing sinful behavior. Draw a line from the word *YES* to the pictures showing the promises God gives us through Jesus. (Also see 2 Corinthians 1:20.) We have these promises as free gifts through faith in Jesus Christ as we are called to repentance and new life in Him by the power of the Holy Spirit working through God's Word and the Sacraments.

On the Way to Canaan

God led the Children of Israel through the desert with a cloud by day and a flame by night.

How does God guide us today?

G___ ___'___ W___ ___ ___

(*A Child's Garden* Bible storybook, pp. 50–51.) The destination for the Children of Israel, as they followed God's guiding cloud and flame, was the promised land of Canaan. The people followed Moses, who was chosen by God. But it was the power of God that provided for their needs, took them across the Jordan River, and defeated Jericho. As God guides us through His Word, our destination is the promised land of heaven. We follow Jesus, who is Himself God and who has the power to defeat sin, death, and Satan through His cross and resurrection.

On the Way to Canaan

Moses

Joshua

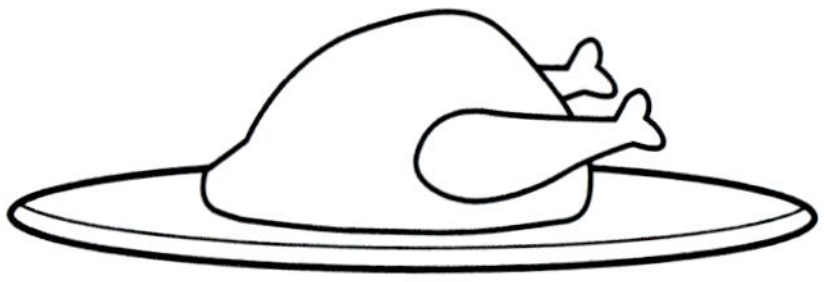

meat

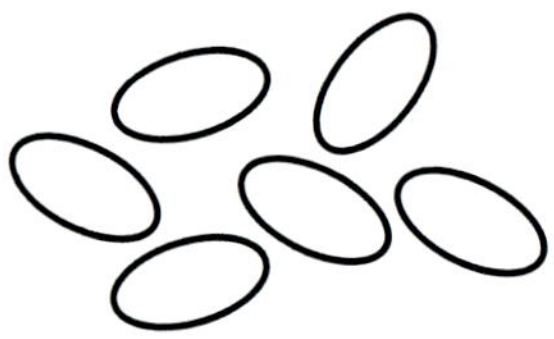

manna

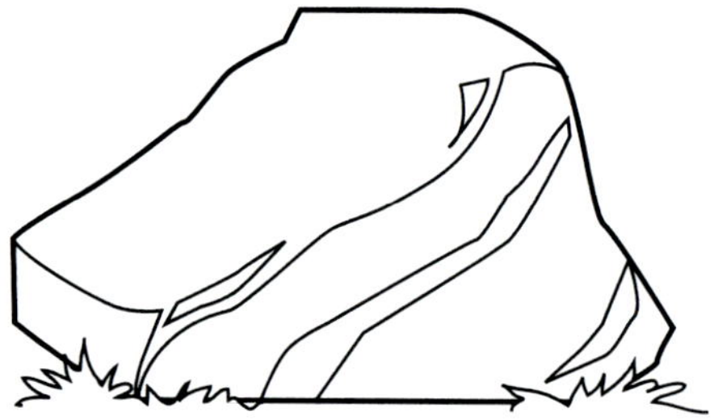

rock

In the mornings, God blessed the people with ________________ to eat.

God also gave them ________________ to eat as they traveled through the desert.

When the people ran out of water, God made water come out of a ________________.

________________ could see the promised land from a mountaintop.

After Moses died, ________________ became the new leader of the Children of Israel.

Directions

(*A Child's Garden* Bible storybook, pp. 50–51.) As you discuss God's provision and care for His people, refer to Luther's explanation of the First Article of the Apostles' Creed, especially the section that says: *[God] richly and daily provides me with all that I need to support this body and life. He defends me against all danger and guards and protects me from all evil. All this He does only out of fatherly, divine goodness and mercy, without any merit or worthiness in me. For all this it is my duty to thank and praise, serve and obey Him. This is most certainly true.*

On the Way to Canaan

The people of Israel traveled through the desert wilderness for many years.

God led them with a cloud during the day and a flame at night.

God gave the people of Israel manna and meat to eat.

Mother buys bread and meat at a grocery store.

When their water was bad, God made it taste good.

One day He made water come out of a rock.

Sometimes the people of Israel complained and were not thankful to God.

Sometimes the people were bad, and God punished them.

One time Moses did not do what God said.

God said, "You shall not go into Canaan."

The first letters of Canaan and Canada are the same.

God told Moses to go up on a mountain.

There Moses saw the new land and then died.

Mount Everest is the tallest mountain in the world.

Joshua became the new leader of the people of Israel.

Joshua led the people into the land of Canaan as God had promised.

Directions

(*A Child's Garden* Bible storybook, pp. 50–51.) Review the Bible lesson as printed on this page, crossing off the sentences that are not related to the Bible story. As you study the stories of the Old Testament, remember that God's love and care remain constant to this day. Malachi 3:6 says, "I the Lord do not change."

Ruth

father	God	Bethlehem
Naomi	Orpah	wheat
Boaz	I	live
sons	Obed	people

Elimelech was the ______________ and ____________ was the mother.

They went to a new land with their two _________________.

Ruth and _______________ were very kind to Naomi.

Ruth said, "Where you go, __________________ will go. Where you live, I will ____________. Your people shall be my _______________. Your God shall be my ________________."

Ruth went back to __________________ with Naomi.

Ruth worked hard gathering _________________ to make bread.

______________ married Ruth. They had a baby boy named

_______________.

Directions

(*A Child's Garden* Bible storybook, pp. 52–53.) Point out that this family had good times and bad times. But no matter what, God was with them. Even though Naomi's husband and sons died, God blessed her with kind and caring Ruth. Even though the women were poor and Ruth had to work hard, God blessed them with Boaz, who gave them extra food and a new family. And years later from their family came God's best blessing of all—our Savior Jesus.

Ruth

God Blessed This Family

God Blesses This Family

(A Child's Garden Bible storybook, pp. 52–53.) Discuss the happy picture at the top of the page. Then have children draw pictures of their families in the blank box and label the names of the people below their pictures. Talk about the ways God blesses us today. Together pray that God will bless families in good times and bad times, and that God will help family members to be kind to each other, forgive one another, and live in harmony and peace, through the grace and blessing of our Lord Jesus Christ.

Directions

Ruth

Ruth showed love to Naomi when she

went back to Bethlehem with her.

would not help Naomi.

worked in the fields for food.

I show love for old people when

I give them my chair when they are standing.

I make lots of noise and run through the house.

I carry heavy boxes for them.

I show love for my parents when

I help them with their work.

I come when they call me.

I let my toys lie all over the floor.

I show love for other boys and girls when

I want to have my way when we play.

I share my toys with them.

I am kind to them.

Directions

(*A Child's Garden* Bible storybook, pp. 52–53.) Ask the children to circle two possible answers for each sentence to indicate ways we can show love and helpfulness to others. Remind the children that we are sinners who do not always do as God wants us to. But God has the power not only to forgive our sins, but also to *transform* our lives. That means He has the power to change us so that we can grow in faith and in living as His children. As we receive the great love of Jesus, we learn to show love to others. 1 John 4:19 says, "We love because He first loved us."

Samuel

Two Very Different Parents

Hannah was a mother who loved her son and loved the Lord. Explain:

____

____

____

____

____

____

Eli was a father who did not do what God wanted him to do. Explain:

____

____

____

____

____

____

Directions

(*A Child's Garden* Bible storybook, pp. 54–55.) Hannah prayed for Samuel, made new clothes for him, and kept her promise to God. Eli saw his sons do wrong and did not stop them. Point out that God wants parents to teach their children to obey His commandments and to know His great love and forgiveness in Jesus. Parents and teachers are doing God's will when they correct mistakes or misbehavior. But like everyone else, they are sinners who do wrong things. They need God's forgiveness and our forgiving love too.

Samuel

Hannah was sad because she had no ______________________.
children—house

She prayed to God. She wanted a baby __________________.
girl—boy

God gave Hannah a son. She called him ____________________.
Moses—Samuel

After a while Hannah brought Samuel to the priest.

His name was ______________________.
Eli—Joseph

One night Samuel heard a voice calling to him.

It was the voice of __________________________.
God—Eli

Samuel told Eli what God had said to him.

Samuel ________________________ God.
obeyed—disobeyed

Eli's sons did not do what Eli told them to do.

Eli's sons ________________________ God.
obeyed—disobeyed

God wants me to hear His word.

He wants me to __________________________ His Word.
obey—disobey

Jesus calls us to repent when we sin.

He wants to ____________________ us.
punish—forgive

Directions

(*A Child's Garden* Bible storybook, pp. 54–55.) Though Hannah and Samuel may seem like the "heroes" of this Bible story, let's remember that it is God who is the hero of everyone's story. It was God who forgave their sins and brought them to faith. It was God who guided them in His ways and led them to live as His people. God is the hero of your story and my story too. God forgives us through Jesus Christ and leads us to faith by the power of the Holy Spirit. It is God's goodness to us, not any goodness on our part, that guides us to live in Him and follow His ways.

Samuel

God wants to talk to us. So, like Samuel, we say:

SPEAK, LORD,
I AM
LISTENING.

God wants us to talk to Him. So, like Hannah, we pray:

____

____

____

____

Directions

(*A Child's Garden* Bible storybook, pp. 54–55.) Have the children color the words spoken by Samuel. Then ask them to write a prayer on the lines or dictate a prayer for a parent or teacher to write down. Suggest that in the prayer they thank God for the many ways He blesses their family. Perhaps also pray for specific help and blessing for each family member. Thank God that through faith in Jesus, we are part of His family, for He has made us children of God! We are children of the heavenly Father, and brothers and sisters in Christ!

David, the Shepherd Boy

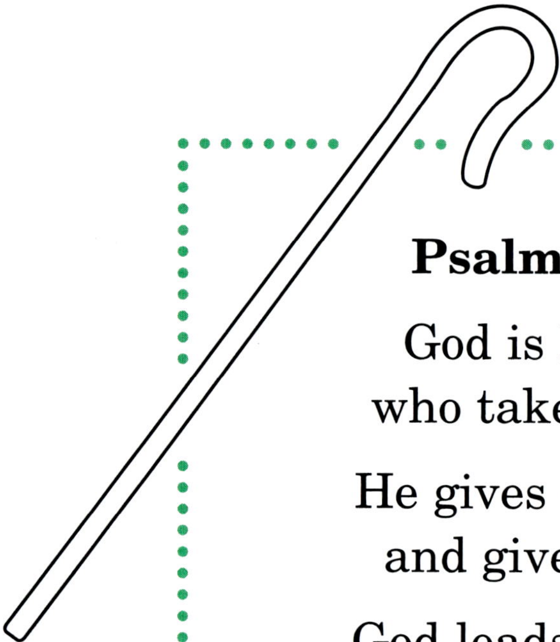

Psalm 23 (paraphrased)

God is like a good shepherd
who takes care of what I need.

He gives me a safe place to rest
and gives me food and drink.

God leads me on the right path,
guiding me to follow His ways.

Even when I am in trouble or danger,
I won't be afraid, because He is with me.

He gives me much more than I need
and blesses me in special ways.

God's loving-kindness
is with me every day
and will be with me always,
even to eternity.

Directions

(*A Child's Garden* Bible storybook, pp. 56–58.) David wrote many songs called psalms. One of the most famous of these compares God to a good shepherd. Discuss characteristics of shepherds and sheep, and compare them to our relationship to God, noting that our vulnerability (as His lambs) and God's care (as our shepherd) are complete. Explain the illustrations of the staff and harp. Then have the children read each verse of the paraphrase, followed by a parent or teacher reading the comparable verse from Scripture.

David, the Shepherd Boy

Who was Saul?

- King of Israel
- Son of Samuel
- Father of David

Who was Goliath?

- A boy
- A king
- A giant

What did Goliath say?

- Do you think I am a dog?
- Do you think I am a child?
- Do you think I am a fool?

What did David say?

- I am afraid.
- I'm bigger and stronger.
- God will help me.

What was in David's sling?

- A stick
- A stone
- A knife

What helped David?

- God's power
- God's grace
- God's protection

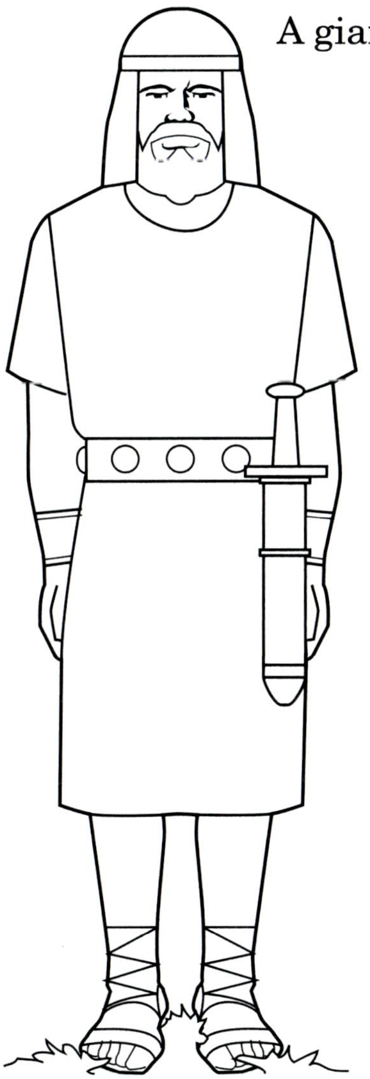

Directions

(*A Child's Garden* Bible storybook, pp. 56–58.) Use the riddles to review David's story. Note that all answers are correct for the last one. As you learn about David's trust in God, emphasize that God is also with us in the problems we may have. When we face troubles, we can say with David, "I come against you in the name of the LORD Almighty" and "the battle is the LORD's" (1 Samuel 17:45, 47). Children today face difficulties and fears that may be large (a physical handicap) or small (a scraped knee). But they can be assured of God's care at all times.

David and Absalom

Who was Absalom?
- The son of Saul
- The son of David
- The king

What did Absalom do?
- Help his father
- Scold the people
- Say bad things about the king

What did Absalom's friends say?
- David is king.
- Do not hurt David.
- Absalom is king.

What did David say?
- Do not hurt Absalom.
- Kill Absalom.
- Let Absalom be king.

Where did the armies meet?
- In the mountains
- In the street
- In a forest

What did David say when Absalom was dead?
- We won!
- I wish I could have died instead.
- He got what he deserved.

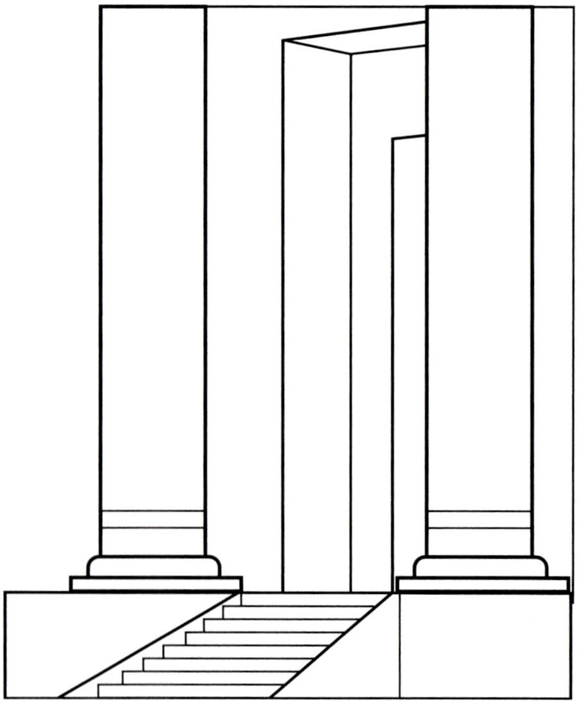

Directions

(*A Child's Garden* Bible storybook, pp. 59–61.) Among other commandments that he broke, Absalom sinned against the Fourth Commandment (disobeyed authorities) and Tenth Commandment (enticed people to turn away from David). Luther's explanations of these commandments say that we should "honor [authorities], serve and obey them" and we should "urge [other people] to stay and do their duty." While David wished he could have died in Absalom's place, we know that Jesus did die in our place, to take away our sins against the Fourth, Tenth, and all other commandments.

David and Absalom

Absalom fought against his ______________________________.

God wants me to ___________________________ the government.

The name of my country is ________________________________.

The leader of my country is _________________________________.

Directions

(*A Child's Garden* Bible storybook, pp. 59–61.) Complete the four sentences on the page. The first answer can be either his *father* or his *king;* either way Absalom was disobedient. The second answer has several possibilities, such as *obey, respect, support,* and *pray for.* After completing the sentences, ask the children to draw their country's flag inside the first flag shape and write a prayer for their country in the second shape. Sing "God Bless Our Native Land." Pray for leaders who love the Lord, for good government, and for peace in the land.

Solomon Builds God's Temple

After David died, his son ______________________ became king.
Absalom—Solomon

Solomon prayed to God. He said, "Please make me a ______________________ king."
wise—rich

God answered his prayer by making him ______________________ than anyone else.
taller—wiser

Solomon built a beautiful ______________________ .
temple—hotel

______________________ of people came to worship at the temple.
Hundreds—Thousands

Solomon prayed, "Lord, this is Your house; hear us when we ______________________ .
pray—work

Solomon built the beautiful temple because he loved ______________ .
money—God

Directions

(*A Child's Garden* Bible storybook, pp. 62–63.) Like Solomon, we often call our church "the house of God" or "God's house." God is everywhere, but we build special buildings to honor Him and to have a place to gather with other believers to worship the Lord. When we go to worship services at church, God speaks to us in His Word. He gives us the blessings of the Sacraments of Baptism and the Lord's Supper. We pray, praise, and thank God in our worship, and we give Him offering gifts to express our love for Him and to share that love with others.

Solomon Builds God's Temple

I Go to God's House

(*A Child's Garden* Bible storybook, pp. 62–63.) Have children draw a picture of their church in the blank space. Or provide a picture of the church, which they may glue in place. Point out that the temple Solomon and his people built was the most beautiful building of their day.

Today we, too, build beautiful churches. We want to honor God by giving Him our best. But more important to God than the look of the church building are the people inside. God desires faithful hearts in His people, who are made His children through Christ Jesus.

Directions

Solomon Builds God's Temple

pulpit candelabra lectern pews (benches)

stained-glass window baptismal font altar

Directions

(*A Child's Garden* Bible storybook, pp. 62–63.) Have children identify the words on this page and draw lines to the matching pictures. Explain that the Third Commandment asks us to set aside one day a week for worship in God's house. We go to worship to learn about Jesus' death and resurrection for our salvation. The Holy Spirit works in our hearts as we receive the means of grace in His Word and Sacraments. And in grateful joy, we respond with thanks and praise, worshiping God in what we say, sing, and do in His holy name.

Elijah and the King

A Spectacular Rescue!

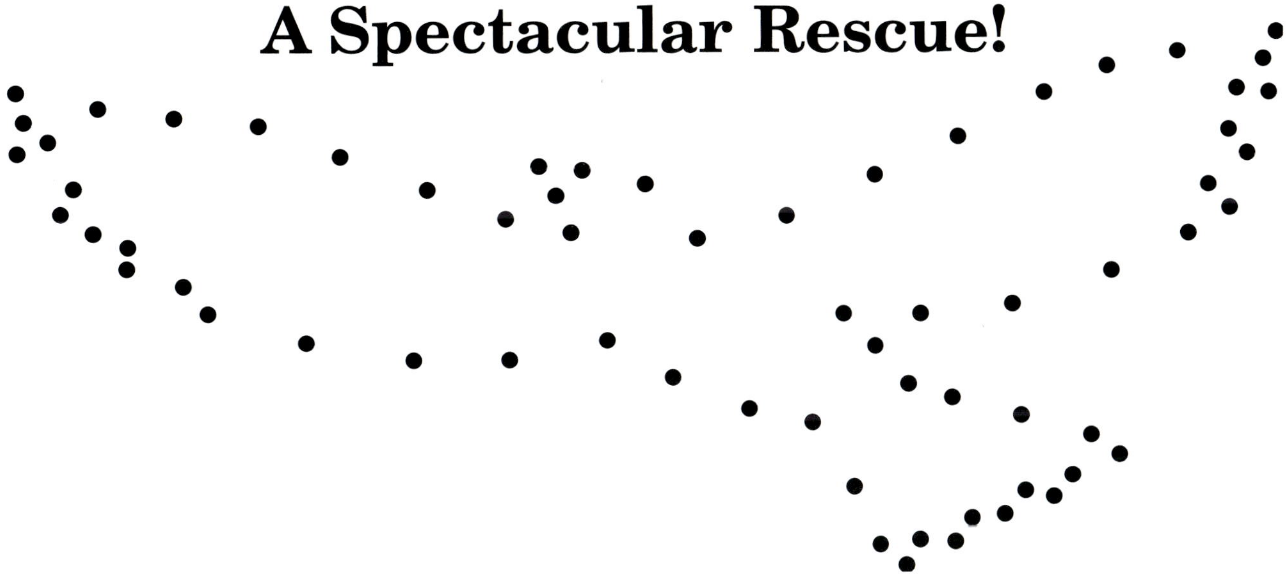

Ravens brought food.

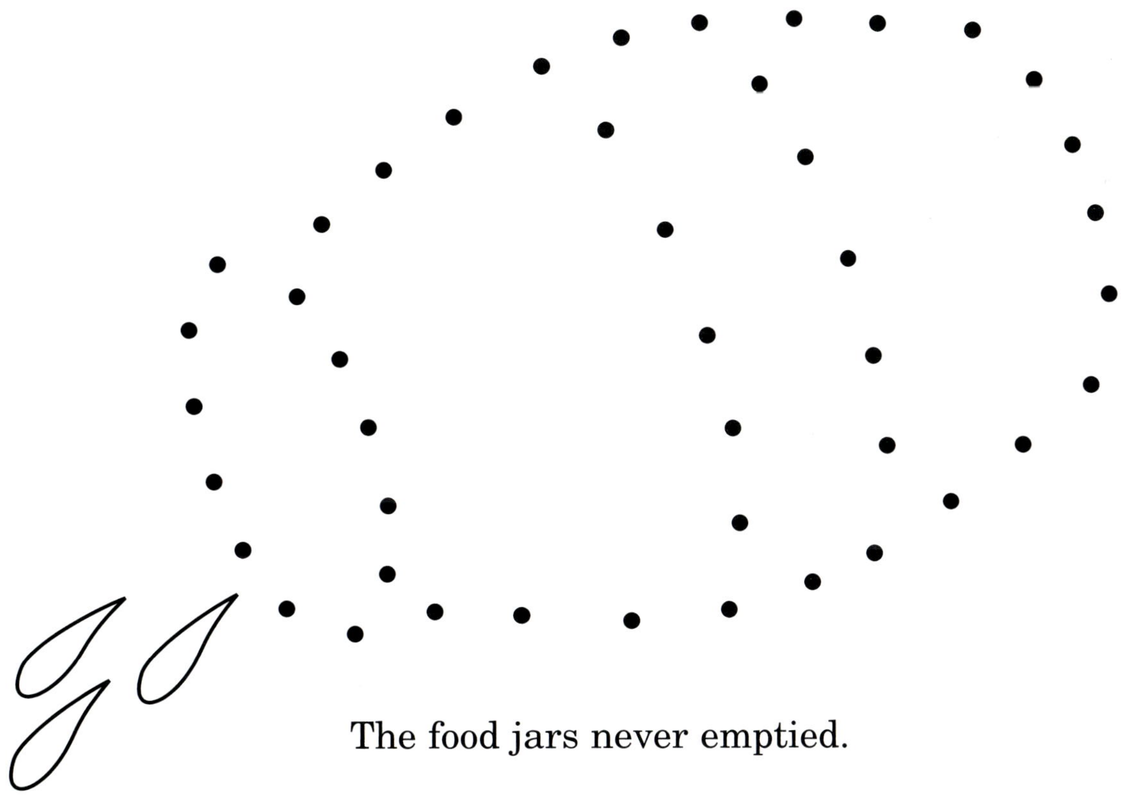

The food jars never emptied.

Directions

(*A Child's Garden* Bible storybook, pp. 64–65.) Trace over the dotted lines as you review God's rescue plan for Elijah. Ask, "Why was Elijah in trouble?" (He had obeyed God's will and confronted the king.) "Why was King Ahab angry?" (He didn't want to admit he was wrong, so he blamed Elijah.) "Why was God angry?" (King Ahab worshiped an idol named Baal.) Then talk about God's greatest rescue plan of all. He sent Jesus to rescue us from sin, death, and the devil. Ask, "How did Jesus do that?" (He died on the cross and arose at Easter for us.)

Elijah and the King

Directions

(*A Child's Garden* Bible storybook, pp. 64–65.) Discuss God's provision through parents who have jobs so they can buy food raised on farms and sold in stores. All of these are blessings from God. The pictures on the left show things as God made them. On the right are things people have made using God's creations. Draw a line to connect the man-made things with the God-made things they were made from. Point out the two man-made items that have no connection with the pictures on the left. Ask which animal supplied the dairy products and leather for shoes.

Elijah and the Prophets of Baal

Prayed to Baal.

Put water on the altar.

Said a simple prayer
to the true God.

Prayed from morning until noon.

Met at Mount Carmel.

Fire came down from heaven.

Said, "O Baal, hear us."

Said, "The Lord is God."

Had no answer to prayer.

Said God would send rain.

Directions

(*A Child's Garden* Bible storybook, pp. 66–67.) Direct the children to draw a line from the beginning of each sentence to the picture it refers to, either the prophets of Baal at the top or Elijah at the bottom. Point out that God worked through the prophet Elijah in amazing ways. God works through His people today, too, though maybe not in such dramatic ways. God can use each child to share the love of God with others and to tell them that Jesus brings us forgiveness, life, and salvation.

Elijah and the Prophets of Baal

Elijah poured [ ] ater on his altar.

God sent fire from [ ] eaven.

The Lord our God [ ] s powerful.

The idol Baal could not [ ] end fire.

The [ ] eople praised God's power.

[ ] lijah's prayer was answered.

God sent [ ] ain for the dry land.

God blessed Elijah in amazing ways! But God also came to Elijah in a gentle ______________________________, a still small voice.

(See 1 Kings 19:12.)

Directions

(*A Child's Garden* Bible storybook, pp. 66–67.) God has amazing power to help us in amazing ways. But He knows what is best and may choose to help us in simple ways that we might not even notice. Encourage the children to observe God's many blessings to us each day. The things we take for granted or may even attribute to "good luck" may be recognized as the blessings of God if we look around us carefully. In prayer ask God to forgive us for Jesus' sake for the times we overlook His blessings and are unthankful. Thank God for His many blessings, those seen and unseen. Fill in the missing letters in the boxes. Write those letters to make a word on the answer line.

Elijah and the Prophets of Baal

(*A Child's Garden* Bible storybook, pp. 66–67.) Have the children write prayer responses the people could say in each pictured situation. Note that one calls for thanks for the amazing blessings of God and the other can thank Him for the quiet blessings He gives to us.

Emphasize that God does not always answer prayers the way we want, but He does answer prayers in the way that is best and at the right time. We can trust His wisdom in all things because He loves us, cares for us, forgives us, and saves us.

Naaman and Elisha

First	"I wish you could go to the prophet in my land."
Next	Naaman was very sick.
Last	A girl worked in his house.

First	Naaman did not want to wash in the river.
Next	Elisha said, "Wash in the Jordan River seven times."
Last	Naaman went to Elisha's house.

First	Naaman finally did what Elisha told him to do.
Next	His servant said, "It is easy to do. Try it."
Last	Naaman's sickness was gone.

First	Elisha did not want any gifts.
Next	The prophet said, "It was God who helped you."
Last	Naaman wanted to pay Elisha for healing him.

Directions

(*A Child's Garden* Bible storybook, pp. 68–70.) In each group, draw lines to show the order in which the sentences happened—first, next, or last. One of the many lessons we can learn from this story is that a child can help grown-ups in important ways. Read 1 Timothy 4:12. Encourage the children to speak to their parents and others about the blessings and care we receive from the Lord. God can work through them to bless the lives of others.

Naaman and Elisha

Naaman lived in the land of Canaan.	**Yes**	**No**
Naaman was a very poor man.	**Yes**	**No**
Naaman was a very sick man.	**Yes**	**No**
The doctors could have helped Naaman.	**Yes**	**No**
A slave girl worked for Naaman.	**Yes**	**No**
The slave girl told Naaman to go to Elisha.	**Yes**	**No**
The prophet said Naaman should wash in the river.	**Yes**	**No**
The name of the river was Jordan.	**Yes**	**No**
Naaman liked what Elisha told him to do.	**Yes**	**No**
Naaman's servant said, "Sometimes an easy thing can help."	**Yes**	**No**
Naaman went to the river and washed himself.	**Yes**	**No**
Naaman washed in the river 17 times.	**Yes**	**No**
Naaman was just as sick as ever.	**Yes**	**No**
Elisha took the gold that Naaman gave him.	**Yes**	**No**
Elisha made Naaman well again.	**Yes**	**No**
The Jordan River made Naaman well again.	**Yes**	**No**
God made Naaman well again.	**Yes**	**No**
God has power to help in sickness.	**Yes**	**No**
When we are sick, we can pray to God for help.	**Yes**	**No**

Directions

(*A Child's Garden* Bible storybook, pp. 68–70.) Read the sentences and circle the word *Yes* if the sentence is correct, or circle *No* if the sentence is wrong. Point out that the hero in this story is not Naaman, not Elisha, and not even the little girl. It was God's action that worked in all of these people. Point out, however, that the girl was helping someone who had not been a friend to her, who had taken her from her homeland and made her a slave. But by God's forgiving, loving, and helpful action in her heart, she was forgiving, loving, and helpful to Naaman.

Naaman and Elisha

Help **ill** **Jesus** **child**

Tender ____________________, meek and mild,

Look on me, a little ____________________.

____________________ me, if it is Thy will,

To recover from all ______________.

Amen.

1. "With God all things are possible" (Matthew 19:26).
2. "Call upon Me in the day of trouble" (Psalm 50:15).
3. "The LORD is good to all; He has compassion on all He has made" (Psalm 145:9).
4. "Give thanks to the LORD, for He is good. His love endures forever" (Psalm 136:1).

_____ God wants us to pray to Him when we have problems.

_____ God will help us because He is loving and kind.

_____ God has power and can help us.

_____ We thank the Lord for blessing us.

Directions

(*A Child's Garden* Bible storybook, pp. 68–70.) Use the bold words in the box at the top of the page to fill in the blanks of the poem prayer. Then read the Bible verses and talk about what they mean. Print the number of each Bible verse before the sentence that helps to explain it. Pray together for people you know who need healing and for all others needing God's grace and blessing.

Three Men in a Furnace

- ☐ A king had a tall idol made of gold.
- ☐ Three men were put in the fire.
- ☐ The king told the people to pray to the idol.
- ☐ The men in the fire were not hurt.
- ☐ The king said, "Your God saved you!"
- ☐ The king said, "Make the fire even hotter."
- ☐ The king saw four men in the fire.
- ☐ The three men would not pray to the gold idol.

Directions

(*A Child's Garden* Bible storybook, pp. 71–73.) Read the sentences and number them from 1 to 8, placing them in the correct order as they happened in the Bible story. Once again God saved His people in an amazing way. But point out that the three men said that even if God did not choose to save them, they would trust in His power and wisdom. We know that whatever may happen to us here, we have the final victory through our Savior, Christ Jesus, who gives us eternal life in heaven. Read 1 Corinthians 15:57.

Three Men in a Furnace

1 3 4 7

The king said, "Pray to the idol when the ______ plays."

Those who did not pray to the idol would die in a ______.

______ men would not pray to the gold idol.

The angry king said, "Make the furnace ______ times hotter and throw them in."

The men trusted in the ______ true God.

The king saw that now there were ______ people in the fire.

When the three men came out of the fire unhurt, their clothes didn't even smell from the ______.

God saves you and me from sin in an amazing way—through the ______ of Jesus.

Directions

(*A Child's Garden* Bible storybook, pp. 71–73.) Direct the children to draw a symbol or number in each box to complete the sentences. Teach the children the names of the three men in the furnace: Shadrach, Meshach, and Abednego. How could the three men be so brave? The power of God blessed them. Pray that God will send you the Holy Spirit to make you strong in faith to live according to God's will. We can do this only through His power working in us. Read 1 Corinthians 12:3b; Acts 16:31; 1 Corinthians 8:6; and Acts 4:12.

Three Men in a Furnace

pray	fear	praise	love	thanks	trust

The First Commandment

You shall have no other gods.

What does this mean? We should ______________, ____________, and ____________ in God above all things.

The Second Commandment

You shall not misuse the name of the Lord your God.

What does this mean? We should fear and love God so that we do not curse, swear, use satanic arts, lie, or deceive by His name, but call upon it in every trouble, _______________, _______________, and give _______________.

We believe in the one true God, the Holy Trinity, Father, Son, and Holy Spirit. God the Father gave us the Ten Commandments to show us His will for our lives. But we fail; we are sinners. So He sent Jesus, God the Son, to rescue us from the punishment of sin. He sends the Holy Spirit to all who believe so that we may grow in faith and grow in living according to His will.

Directions

(*A Child's Garden* Bible storybook, pp. 71–73.) Have the children complete Luther's explanations of the First and Second Commandments, using the words in the answer box to fill in the blanks. The First and Second Commandments are key factors in this Bible story. Shadrach, Meshach, and Abednego could not keep God's commands perfectly because they were sinners like us. But by the grace of God they received faith and forgiveness and were strengthened by God to follow God's will. Pray that God would also strengthen you in faith.

Daniel and the Lions

- [ ] Some people were jealous of Daniel because he was an important leader.
- [ ] The king got up early the next morning to see if Daniel was all right.
- [ ] The people asked the king to make a law that everyone should pray to the king.
- [ ] God sent an angel to close the lions' mouths.
- [ ] Daniel did not obey the law. He prayed to the true God.
- [ ] The king was sorry he made such a foolish law, but it could not be changed.
- [ ] Daniel was thrown into the lions' den.
- [ ] The king said, "The God of Daniel is the true God."

Directions

(*Child's Garden* Bible storybook, pp. 74–75.) Read the sentences and number them from 1 to 8, placing them in the correct order as they happened in the Bible story. This story is about the faithfulness of God to His people. In Joshua 23:14, the Bible says, "You know with all your heart and soul that not one of all the good promises the LORD your God gave you has failed. Every promise has been fulfilled; not one has failed." Any faithfulness that Daniel or we evidence in our lives is a fruit of the Holy Spirit working in us. See Galatians 5:22.

Daniel and the Lions

One evening Katie was home alone with her teenage sister Christine. The TV was off, Katie was playing with her teddy bear, and Christine was reading a book.

Katie was very quiet. She looked as if she would soon cry. She said to her sister, "I don't like to be alone. I'm afraid."

"Why, Katie," said Christine, "we are not alone. God sends His angels to guard us. They are all around us."

Katie wanted to hear more about angels. She said, "I can't see them. Are they here in this room?"

Christine put down her book and said, "There are many, many angels, not just one or two. And the angels are very strong. God gives them much power.

"The angels do what God tells them to do. In the Bible we read that they often carried messages from God to people on earth."

Katie sat up happily and said, "Like at Christmas! The angel came to tell the shepherds that the Savior was born in Bethlehem!"

"Right," said Christine. "God also tells the angels to care for us here on earth. We cannot see them, but they are here, our guardian angels, protecting us."

Katie sat on the sofa next to her sister and said, "That's like the story of Daniel! God sent an angel to protect him too!"

"And someday," Christine added, "we will hear the angels that stand at the throne of God singing His praises."

"We will?" Katie asked.

"Yes," said Christine, "we will join the angels in praising God when we are in heaven. And we know we are going there because Jesus promises salvation to all who believe in Him!"

Directions

A Child's Garden Bible storybook, pp. 74–75.) Read the story and use a yellow crayon to highlight all the sentences that give information about angels. *Note: People's imaginations have created a lot of myths about angels. For example, it is not true that people become angels. We need to look to the Bible for the truth.* Emphasize that though Bible stories happened long ago, they teach us about God's love for us today, because God does not change. As the Bible says in Hebrews 13:8, "Jesus Christ is the same yesterday and today and forever."

The Morning Prayer

I thank You, my heavenly Father,
through Jesus Christ, Your dear Son,
that You have kept me this night
from all harm and danger;
and I pray that You would keep me
this day also from sin and every evil,
that all my doings and life may please You.
For into Your hands I commend myself,
my body and soul, and all things.
Let Your holy angel be with me,
that the evil foe may
have no power over me.
Amen.

Directions

(*A Child's Garden* Bible storybook, pp. 74–75.) This prayer, by Martin Luther, is good to use at the beginning of each day. It speaks of God's constant care for us, His protection of us through His holy angels, and of the Savior, Jesus, who has rescued us from the evils of sin, death, and Satan. May God bless You always in Christ Jesus!